Windmills
of
Suffolk

Published by

Dean Regan-1997

Forward

As strange as it may seem this book was not initially borne out of any great love of either Windmills or indeed of the county of Suffolk. It started with the long standing ambition to put together a collection of my drawings and paintings in a modest publication. I had in mind two aims with this book, the first was to satisfy myself that I could produce artwork to a standard that would be of interest to others and secondly, perhaps selfishly, to see my own work in print on the shelf of a bookshop.

In 1995 I had recently moved back to Suffolk with my job and started to paint and draw some of the subjects that I saw on my daily journeys across the county, the realisation gradually dawned on me that I had the material for a book right in front of me.

It was whilst driving along the A12 to the north of Woodbridge on a summers evening in 1996 that I glimpsed the wonderful sight of the turning sails of Buttram's mill, and in that instant this book began.

Now, one year on, the paintings, sketches and notes are complete and displayed in this little book. Most of the illustrations were drawn with black ink technical pens on A3 size Bockingford watercolour paper and took between four and ten hours each to complete.

Index to Illustrations

Contents

Acknowledgements

This first book is dedicated to the following for their unending patience and encouragement during the past year,

Hilary and Hannah.

My colleagues and friends.

Those dedicated people who maintain the mills for future generations.

Windmills of Suffolk - Dean Regan 1997

Printed by

Fuller-Davies Ltd
Unit 22
Riverside Industrial Park
IPSWICH
Suffolk

Chapter One

Post Mills

It is not clear whether the windmill was invented in this country or an idea imported from abroad, there are several theories that would have them originating as far away as China or the Middle East.

The Doomsday Book makes no reference to a windmill of any description, it would seem reasonable however to assume that they were developed to meet the needs of agriculture. The earliest reference to a windmill in England dates from 1185 and during the 13th century windmills spread throughout England, numbering up to 10,000 by the end of the century.

In Suffolk, records show more than 700 in operation during the 18th century with 430 still working in 1838.

These early mills were known as Post mills, the name is derived from the massive central oak post about which the whole mill could be turned to face the wind. The very early mills would consist of this vertical post supported by a base of two cross trees and braced by four quarter bars joining the top of the post to the extremities of the cross trees, atop the post would be mounted the windshaft angled slightly up from the horizontal. At the forward end of the windshaft were mounted the sails.

The cross trees themselves were often buried in the earth to provide stability, but the principle of the post mill was that it could be moved when required.

Later during the early 16th century when these mills had become very large permanent structures, a body or buck was added to give protection to the miller and the corn. During the early 18th century round-houses were added to provide extra storage space and to provide protection for the structure of the mill.

The buck was usually weather-boarded and painted white, all of those surviving in Suffolk are preserved in this way. Entrance to the buck is through a door to the rear, from a small platform at the top of a flight of steps, the steps themselves being joined to the buck, the whole assembly turning around the post. The round-house was in no way joined to the mill or buck, usually built of brick, some still remain that are of clay lump or of flint, quite often the round-house would be plastered on the inside and rendered on the outside. A conical roof of wooden boards covered with felt or perhaps tiles would extend underneath the buck to the point where the post protruded up through into the buck.

It was normal practice for a round-house to have two doors on the ground floor, normally on opposite sides to allow access no matter what the wind direction. Several millers were killed by the silently turning sails through using the wrong door when the wind had changed direction!

Some round-houses took on huge proportions, those at Thorndon and Friston being among the largest, whilst that at Saxstead Green was raised three times during it's lifetime. The Post mill at Drinkstone survived without a round-house at all for two hundred years. Several of these have been converted to dwellings and two that remain have thatched roofs.

Occasionally the mill was moved to a new location and a new round-house built, as at Thorpeness, though in this case it is rectangular and is in use as a tourist information office.

All Post mills drove at least one pair of millstones, some of the larger mills drove four pairs.

Drinkstone

1689

TL 964622

This diminutive post mill, the oldest to survive in Suffolk, has worked for the best part of two and a half centuries, much of that time without the benefit of a round-house and largely in the ownership of the Clover family.

Now in need of new sails (only two remain) the buck and round-house are intact, the round-house is beautifully constructed of brick and flint. Starting its life with four common sails, i.e. canvas spread over wooden frames, these were replaced in the 19th century with spring sails for a while and eventually ending with two spring and two common sails.

The buck has been extended fore and aft and the original tail pole was replaced by a fantail in 1940 to turn the mill into wind automatically.

Its life has not been without incident, during one storm the whole windshaft and sails were thrown forward, with the rear of the shaft ripping up through the buck roof. In 1963 a replacement fantail was fitted from the old mill at nearby Woolpit, which was then demolished.

An interesting feature is that the sails do not have the usual twist along their length but are simply inclined at an angle to allow the wind to turn them.

Framsden

1760

TM 192598

A fine restored post mill stands high on a hill dominating the tiny village of Framsden. It is, at forty eight feet, the second tallest of the post mills standing in the county today.

Built in 1760, it had a very different appearance then from that of today. There was no brick round-house and the sails were of the canvas and wood type, the mill was turned into wind by means of a tail pole.

In 1836 the mill was raised eighteen feet and the brick round-house was built, also at this time a fantail and steps were added. The wooden windshaft was replaced by an iron one which then carried four large patent (shuttered) sails.

The mill finally ceased to work in the 1930's and then gradually became derelict until 1966 when a group of volunteers started work on restoration. Two new patent sails were fitted in 1969 and in 1972 a new fantail was fitted.

At present the mill has only two sails though is functional in all other respects. It is privately owned, though it can be clearly observed from the gate way thirty metres away.

Friston

1811

TM 412601

The tallest Post mill in England, the white weather-boarded buck can be seen from the main Snape to Aldeburgh road. It has dominated this skyline for over one hundred and fifty years.

The most unusual event in this mills history must be the fact that although originally erected on mill hill in Woodbridge as one of four, it was moved in 1812 to its present site.

The mill continued to work with the power of the wind until 1956, although it had lost a pair of sails in 1943. After 1956 it continued to grind with the aid of a small diesel engine. It should be noted that a mill losing a sail or two could still operate with only one pair, though the power to the millstones would be reduced to about sixty percent of that with four sails.

In its heyday the mill ran three pairs of stones, employing three millers and a caner.

The mighty round-house and buck are preserved but the stones have been removed and the sails and fantail have gone.

Holton St Peter

1749

TM 403773

A beautiful little post mill sits high above the pretty village of Holton to the East of Halesworth.

Resplendent in the usual Suffolk livery of white weather-boarded buck and white common sails, it appears perfect in every way. A great deal of care has gone into the restoration of this mill, although situated on private land it is maintained by Suffolk County Council and a winding footpath is provided up the hill through the grounds of the old mill house (itself a gem of Suffolk architecture).

The steep walk up from the village is well worth the effort, the mill is open on certain bank holidays throughout the year and the visitor is rewarded with a feeling of moving back to a more peaceful, simpler age.

The mill itself once carried two common sails and two spring sails as at Drinkstone, though now has four lightweight common sails with hollow stocks to reduce the weight on the windshaft, this unfortunately means the sails will never turn. The fantail is a huge affair and is fully functional, moving the mill around constantly on a breezy day. The round-house is brick with a covering of black tar for weather proofing and though only one storey high, has been excavated inside to provide two storey's.

Saxmundham

1824

TM 383631

Once a dominating feature, this mill was gradually surrounded by the market town of Saxmundham and though raised several times to regain wind, due to the increasing proximity of houses, it ceased work in 1907.

The round-house survives but only just, for many years it has been in use as a store as part of garage premises. With the demise of the garage it has fallen into disrepair and urgent action is now required to save it. The roof is rotten and much of it has fallen in, the property is for sale.

When working this mill was at least as high as that of the post mill at Friston.

Saxstead Green

1796

TM 253644

Perhaps the finest example of a post mill in the World, the mill at Saxstead Green is maintained in magnificent condition by Suffolk County Council.

The sails can regularly be seen turning whenever there is a light breeze, the six bladed fantail is painted in the traditional Suffolk blue scheme. Visitors are welcomed during the summer months and there can be few better ways to spend a summers afternoon than a lunch at the pub just across the green and a tour of the mill.

The earliest reference to a mill on the green is in 1287, the present mill started life with four common sails and a single pair of stones, she was turned into wind with a tail pole and the round-house was only eight feet tall at the eaves. Since then the mill has been raised three times to her present height.

Between 1957 and 1960 the mill was dismantled and completely refurbished, any timbers not in perfect condition were replaced and some of the shutters in the sails removed to prevent damage to the sails in high winds.

Snape

1668

TM 394583

The mill at Snape was dismantled in 1933 though its spirit lives on in the form of its beautifully converted round-house, located just off the main Woodbridge to Leiston road in the village it can be seen from the public footpath.

The second illustration depicts the mill as it was in 1907 towards the end of its working life, unusually this mill was also used for wood turning.

Benjamin Britten, the famous composer, lived in the round-house for a while.

The round-house is a perfect example of how an old mill can live on, despite the passing of its original purpose, as I live close to Snape I often drive through the village and can never resist the urge to glance through the open gateway at the mill.

The upper storey must give a fabulous view of the famous maltings half a mile away to the south.

Stratford St Andrew
1824

TM 356602

Few records remain to indicate the history of this modest round-house. The machinery and buck have gone and the two storey brick round-house is presently in use as a summer-house.

It is pleasantly located, surrounded by a lawn in the garden of a house just to the north of the village church off the main A12 road.

Stanton
1791

TL 971733

High on a hill to the north of the village the mill is preserved in very good condition, a typical Suffolk post mill with its white weather-boarded buck, four sails and its brick round-house.

The mill was unusual in that it had an eight bladed fantail or fly, during the war the buck was painted grey to prevent enemy aircraft using it as a navigation mark for attacking nearby airfields.

Syleham

1823

TM 214777

The little post mill was originally erected 2 miles away at Wingfield Green in 1730 along side another post mill. In 1820 both mills were acquired by Robert Sparkes and he, believing that one mill was taking the wind away from the other, moved this mill to its present position in 1823.

The two common and two spring sails drove two pairs of French burr stones, and later, a third pair were added in the round-house powered by a small oil engine.

In 1936 the mill narrowly avoided catastrophe when it was struck by lightning whilst the miller was inside. The mill continued to work using the wind until 1951 and then with the oil fired engine until 1967.

By 1974 the mill was in need of some repair with only one pair of sails, a grant was received from the council, however the mill is now in a very poor state and is probably beyond any chance of survival.

The buck is completely derelict and much of the round-house rendering is missing exposing the clay lump walls.

Thorndon

1797

TM 139698

When complete with its buck Thorndon mill was the tallest post mill in Suffolk, the round-house survives in fairly good order.

Though not shown on any current map a colleague living in the village of Occold brought this mill to my attention. As he regularly passes through Thorndon village whilst out jogging, and mindful of my interest in windmills, he plucked up the courage to suggest that this odd round building may once have been a mill. The vital clue he had missed was on the gate leading to the round-house, a very neat sign inscribed 'Mill Farm'.

The mill continued to work until 1923 when it was struck by lightning and ruined.

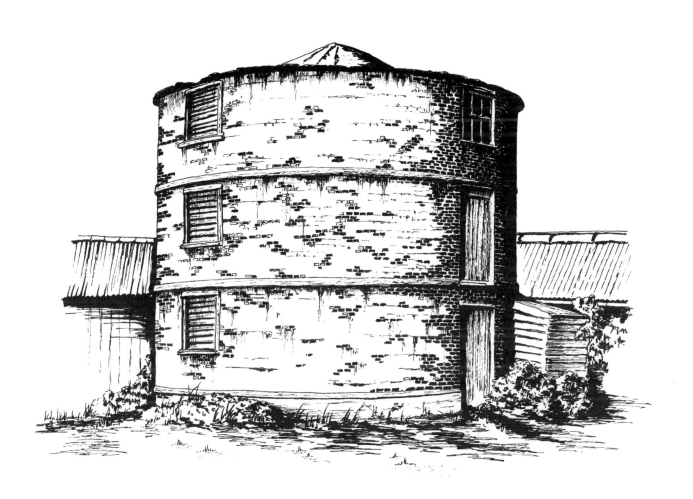

Thorpeness

1922

TM 468598

Built by Whitmores of Wickham Market, this fine mill was first erected in the neighbouring village of Aldringham in 1803 for the purpose of grinding corn.

In the 1890's it was bought by the Ogilvy family and in 1922-1923 was moved to the new holiday village of Thorpeness to begin a new lease of life as a windpump.

The water is drawn from a twenty eight foot deep well located below the round-house, the new round-house is not in fact round but rectangular and also contains an auxiliary pumping engine, the roof is of red clay pantiles and the walls of white painted blocks. The council have set up a tourist information office in the round-house which is open on bank holidays and afternoons during August.

Any visitor to the mill cannot fail to see the odd structure beside the mill, known as the 'House in the Clouds', this is in fact the village water tower, built on stilts and clad in painted weather-boarding it has accommodation for ten persons and is available for rent as a holiday home.

Perhaps the most interesting story concerning this structure is the 'friendly fire' incident, one night during the second world war, the anti-aircraft guns on the heath were firing at incoming V2 rockets when they accidently hit the water tower.

The two old ladies living in the bedroom beneath it slept through the whole episode, unfortunately with steel in short supply the tank had to be mended with one of its own panels thus reducing its capacity from 50,000 to 30,000 gallons!

The mill was in use pumping water up to the tank until 1940 when it was superseded by an engine, in turn this was itself made redundant when the village was joined to the water mains in 1963. During this time the mill deteriorated, being damaged in the storm of 1972 which sent the fantail or 'fly' crashing to the ground and in 1974 it was damaged by a heath fire.

The mill stands in very pleasant surroundings, on a small grassy rise next to the golf course, with park benches provided on three sides facing the mill, it is a favourite site for a family picnic on a sunny day.

I well remember the time when my wife left her handbag on one of the benches, some time later she received a telephone call from the staff at the golf course hotel to say that someone had handed it in to them. When she collected it later everything was still in the bag. This must surely say something about the sort of people who visit windmills.

Darsham

1783

TM 415702

Originally occupying a site nearby in the same village, this mill was moved to its present location in 1801. When working she drove three pairs of stones, two in the head of the buck and the third pair in the tail.

Although not on any map I glimpsed the conical thatched roof from a distance and was pleasantly surprised to find such a well preserved round-house situated on a sunlit grassy knoll overlooking the village.

The construction of the round-house suggests that the mill itself was raised at least once during its lifetime as the lower of the two storey's is of flint whilst the upper is of brick, the addition of the thatched roof completely compliments the character of the building.

Chapter Two

Smock Mills

A variation of the more numerous tower mill, they are, because of their appearance, said to take their name from the old farmers smock of the late 17th century.

The mills were tapered in profile, usually with a brick base and a wooden flat sided tower, this tower was usually octagonal and covered with horizontal weather-boarding. These mills had a cap similar to that of the tower mills. Early versions were winded by tail pole as at Herringfleet, though the later mills had fantails mounted at the rear of the cap.

The advent of the Smock mill was a major advancement in milling, as now the only part of the mill that rotated to face the wind was the cap, which contained the windshaft assembly and the sails. The milling machinery was contained within the tower and access was gained from a door at the ground floor. The weather-boarding was normally painted white though several were tarred black, a few had as many as twelve sides.

Setting the common sails presented much the same problem to the miller as those of the post mill in that the canvas had to be un-furled across each sail in turn, this task was by necessity performed with the brake off and it was not uncommon for the sails to begin to turn whilst the miller was still on a sail frame!

The advent of the self regulating shuttered sail overcame the need for canvas to be spread but, until this time, a stage was normally built around the tower of the smock to enable the miller to set the sails, again two doors were provided on opposite sides of the gallery to allow access with the wind from any direction.

Of course a drawback was that the mill was no longer able to be moved from one location to another, the other more serious problem was that of water ingress to the wooden structure of the tower. As the mill was multi-sided the edges of the weatherboards were open to the elements and so were vulnerable to dampness. It is largely due to this design fault that most of these mills have not survived. Those that do still exist today do so due to constant care and usually with the aid of the local authority as they are all buildings of historic interest.

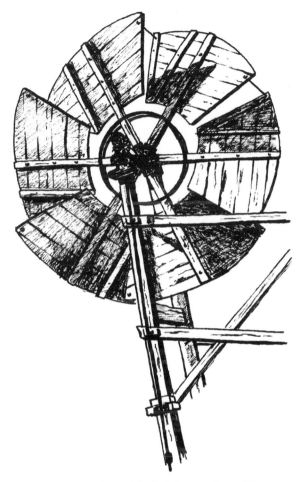

A typical six bladed fantail or 'fly'.

Dalham

1802

TL 719617

This very imposing structure last worked in 1926. It was certainly the largest smock mill in the county at a height of fifty feet.

As with many of these mills, once she had stopped working she started to deteriorate and by 1935 was in need of urgent maintenance, the fantail had gone and the shutters had been removed from the sails. By 1938 much work had been completed and the mill was again in good order. Again her condition deteriorated until 1972 when she was bought by Frank Farrow, who with the aid of the County Council and the Historic buildings Council has done much work in restoring her to her present condition.

Though still without sails she is a wonderful sight, resplendent in horizontal white weather-boarding after many years clad in vertical boards. If any of these mills deserves to be restored to original condition then this is surely the one.

Drinkstone

1689/1780

TL 964621

In the shadow of the neighbouring post mill one hundred yards to the north, this little smock mill is in mid restoration with a new covering of weather-proof sheeting and battens to take the weather-boarding.

There has been a mill on this site for many centuries, the present smock mill is built on the foundations of an earlier horse driven mill that was erected in 1689. She has a sunken basement which is plastered on the inside and was originally winded by a chain winch as at Herringfleet and in later years by a fly (fantail).

Towards the end of her working life a pair of common sails together with a pair of spring sails were in use, then a small oil fired engine was used until the mill finally ceased work.

Great Thurlow

1807

TL 672500

Known as 'Collis' mill this little smock mill, built on the site of an earlier post mill, is situated to the West of the county and is in near perfect condition. A small grassed area surrounds the mill and access can be gained via a public footpath from the main road fifty yards away.

Covered in black tarred weather-boards, she is complete with four common sails and a fantail.

During her working life it was possible to see thirteen other mills working from her stage at the rear of the cap. She is, unfortunately, the only survivor. Unusually for a smock mill she was moved from Slough in Buckinghamshire in 1807.

The mill continued to work until 1924 with the assistance of an auxiliary engine at which time the sails were removed. The mill gradually became derelict until 1959 when the new owners started restoration, this work was completed in 1962 with new fantail, sails and cap.

Herringfleet

1826

TM 466976

This beautiful black tarred smock mill stands isolated beside the river Waveney. A marsh drainage mill, it is the last of its type surviving in this country.

Finishing her working life 1956, she was transferred to the ownership of the County Council in 1958. In perfect condition, the mill is allowed to turn on occasions throughout the year and apart from the odd interruption from the nearby railway line, the scene is much the same as it was when the mill was erected.

The mill is winded by a tailpole chain winch, this meant that with the sails set, the marshman would need to be in attendance constantly to ensure the sails were facing into wind. The method of rotating the cap was to connect the end of the chain to one of twelve posts set in the ground around the mill, the marsh man would then wind the winch handle to pull the tailpole towards the post thus rotating the cap.

The windshaft is connected to a scoop wheel sixteen feet in diameter. The Mill contains a fireplace and a wooden settle, these were provided for the comfort of the marshman during the long winter nights.

Walton

1804

TM 290345

As recently as 1995 this mill was listed in the Historic buildings at risk register at the Suffolk County Council records office. It was in a state of near collapse with most of the weatherboarding missing and the cap gone, the interior was open to the elements and it must surely have been near to demolition.

With this information in mind I approached its location believing that there would be little left to sketch, it was to my surprise to find the tower repaired, with brickwork intact and fine new white painted boarding and cap.

It is believed that this mill was known as Wadgate mill and when newly erected it served not only to grind corn , but also as a navigation marker for mariners along the Orwell.

Chapter Three

Tower Mills

A development of the smock and post mill, the tower mill was constructed with a brick tower, there being no stone locally available, as with the smock mill, the only part of the mill that turned to face the wind was the cap.

The very first tower mill was in fact erected at Dover in 1295. Early tower mills were modest in height with two or three floors and the cap was rotated by a tailpole.

The later towers were built with the windshaft inclined above the horizontal, this enabled the tower to be built with a 'batter', i.e. to reduce in girth towards the top of the tower. This provided increased storage space at the base and was inherently more stable. Of course the towers were usually cylindrical to allow the sails to clear the structure, though a few are known to have been erected with flat sides.

In Suffolk tower mills were mainly built to grind corn or animal feed as opposed to those in Norfolk where a great many are still to be seen standing as drainage mills.

The great advantage of the tower mill was that the machinery was fixed in place so an auxiliary engine could be installed to drive the stones on a day with little or no wind.

These mills normally had four patent or shuttered sails, with either a six or eight bladed fly, in other parts of the country, tower mills had as many as ten sails, some superb examples of multi-sailed tower mills survive in Lincolnshire where as the six sailed mills of Suffolk have all gone.

The tallest tower mill in the county stood at one hundred feet, with eleven floors, and was built in Great Yarmouth in 1812. Named High mill, it was in perfect condition when it was demolished in 1904.

Those tower mills that have survived have generally done so without their sails and caps, though a few fine examples still remain such as Buttram's mill at Woodbridge and Pakenham mill near the village of Ixworth.

Bardwell

1823

TL 941737

A relatively small mill, she has been without sails or fly since 1925 but retains her original cap and machinery and still grinds today, powered by an auxiliary engine. From the evidence of old photographs she was a beautifully proportioned little tower mill with four patent shuttered sails and weather-boarded cap with finial.

The first mill to have been erected on this site was in 1283 and it is thought that a mill has been located on this site ever since then. Certainly records show evidence of a previous smock mill and before that a post mill.

Perhaps my greatest achievement whilst producing these illustrations was when a friend looking at the one of Bardwell recognised the little car in the mill yard as a metro.

Bardwell

Burgh

1842

TM 230514

This large mill stands high on top of a hill in the village of Burgh to the north of Woodbridge overlooking the village of Grundisburgh. Though one of the nearest mills to my home it was without doubt one of the most difficult to observe because of its secluded position.

The largest of the mills built by Whitmores of Wickham Market and originally painted black and white she was a very powerful mill, driving four pairs of stones in a strong wind. The mill contained seven floors and measured fifty seven feet to the base of the cap. The ground floor has an inside diameter of twenty three feet, narrowing to thirteen at the top.

The sails were removed in 1919 and an eight horse power engine was installed with a belt drive to the third floor to drive the stones. Like many other mills around the county she is built on the site of an earlier mill.

As can be seen from the drawing she provides her present owner with possibly the best television signal in the county.

Buxhall

1860

TL 998577

Built on the foundations of a smock mill, the walls of the tower are vertical to the third floor. It is believed the builder was William Bear. A very modern mill, it had many of the latest innovations for its time. The cap was fitted with an iron gutter to collect rain water and the sails were exceptional in having eleven bays of three shutters each and measured eighty feet in span, they were also fitted with Robert Catchpole's 'sky scraper' air brakes which were used to slow the sails down.

Cockfield

1891

TL 904539

The last windmill to be built in Suffolk, she worked for only nine years. Built by Brewer and Sillitoe of Long Melford to replace an earlier tower mill on the same site known as the 'Pepper mill'.

Now in use as a dwelling, the black tarred tower remains without cap or sails.

Gazeley

1844

TL 717649

Situated to the extreme west of the county, like so many others only the tower remains and it has been put to good use as a dwelling.

Built by Mr William Death she ceased to grind in 1910. During her working life she drove up to five pairs of stones, three pairs of which could be driven by an engine that had been installed in 1880.

Great Welnetham

1865

TL 878598

Known as the 'Tutelina Mill' the tower is situated to the west of the Lavenham to Bury St Edmunds road just as you enter the village from the south. Though without her sails and cap the little mill and nearby barn make an attractive site and was a pleasure to illustrate.

The mill was still known to be working in 1900, though had lost her sails in a gale in 1916. (page 58)

Great Welnetham

Kelsale

1856

TM 382647

Located to the east of the A12 trunk road that by-passes Saxmundham, this grey tower was built by Whitmores of Wickham Market and like the tower mill at Burgh, was originally finished in a livery of black and white paint.

With seven floors and standing at fifty five feet she was a powerful mill and replaced a post mill that stood in the same yard, now she lives on, converted to a house.

Pakenham

1831

TL 931694

Competing with Buttram's mill at Woodbridge for the title of best preserved tower mill in the county, this black tarred mill is certainly worth a visit. Still producing flour on occasion from her three pairs of stones.

A near disaster was averted by the miller in 1947 when she became tail winded in a gale and in 1971 she was struck by lightning, only being saved by the sack hoist chain which touched the ground.

Stansfield

Stansfield

1840

TL 785528

Little is known of the history of this mill, though it is known that the cap was removed in 1922 and that it replaced another mill on the same site. It is in very poor condition and though a public footpath runs past it the way is barred by a gate to the private grounds of the mill house.

Thelnetham

1819

TM 011790

Replacing a post mill on the same site overlooking the Norfolk border, this superb little tower mill is still working on some weekends and bank holidays throughout the summer months. Black tarred with white cap and sails, the fly is painted in the original red, white and blue. She is maintained by a dedicated group of enthusiasts and flour produced at the mill can be bought in the village shop. Definitely a mill to visit.

Thelnetham

Chilton Street

1846

TL 757472

Completely derelict, little is known of this red brick tower except the fact that it stands on or near the site of a mill built in 1216, in the reign of Henry III.

Walberswick

1897

TM 487737

A little red brick marsh drainage mill occupying an isolated spot about one mile to the south of the seaside village of Walberswick. It has suffered much abuse over the years including being used as a coastal gunnery target during the war and though substantially rebuilt was then victim to a malicious fire in the 1960's.

If nothing else it provides an interesting navigation point for those walking through the tall reeds of the surrounding marshes.

Aldeburgh

1824

TM 465560

Known as Fort Green mill, this tower was converted into a house in 1902. It is without doubt one of the most interesting subjects that I have drawn.

Buttram's

Buttram's

1836

TM 264493

This fully restored tower mill, named after a long standing family of millers stands in the town of Woodbridge and was without doubt the inspiration for this book.

Built by the firm of Whitmores of Wickham Market, she is fitted with fully shuttered patent sails and a six bladed fly. The sails are to be seen turning on any day with a stiff breeze and the mill is open to the public, with a tour guide from the County Council usually on hand to lead the visitor up through the six floors or to discuss the excellent display on the ground floor. Privately owned, she is maintained by her owner and the County Council.

Last working commercially in 1928 she is no longer allowed to grind to prevent damage to the machinery, the keen observer will notice that one pair of sails is shorter than the other.

Trickers   1815   TM 268491

Located just to the south of Buttram's this tower is now in use as a common room and accommodation, as part of a development for handicapped people, it ceased work in 1920.

Trickers

Conclusion

Thirty three windmills, not much to fill a book, but the quantity is not important. I hope having reached this page that you might agree with me that the few that are left are worth preserving, they are surely a porthole into a past age.

From the splendour of Saxstead Green or Buttram's to the dereliction of Chilton Street they seem to fire the imagination. I hope my efforts have in some small way done them justice. Perhaps I should feel a sadness at having reached the end of this task but, far from that, I feel a great sense of achievement at helping to educate others in an important part of our history.

If I have missed a windmill out there I apologise, perhaps in a while I will have another look and include it in a reprint but for now I have my eye on the Farm houses and barns of the county.

Artists note
Though normally busy with my full time career as a pilot, I am always willing to take on a private commission in Ink or watercolour for a reasonable sum and perhaps include it in a future book.

Locations of Suffolk Windmills

1	Gazeley	*16*	Saxstead Green
2	Stansfield	*17*	Framsden
3	Dalham	*18*	Burgh
4	Great Thurlow	*19*	Buttram's/Trickers
5	Chilton Street	*20*	Snape
6	Great Welnetham	*21*	Friston
7	Cockfield	*22*	Thorpeness
8	Buxhall	*23*	Saxmundham
9	Drinkstone	*24*	Orford
10	Bardwell	*25*	Darsham
11	Stanton Upthorpe	*26*	Walberswick
12	Pakenham	*27*	Holton St Peter
13	Thelnetham	*28*	Southwold
14	Syleham	*29*	Herringfleet
15	Thorndon		